# SNAKES

# SNAKES

by Sylvia A. Johnson

Photographs by Modoki Masuda

A Lerner Natural Science Book

Lerner Publications Company • Minneapolis

**Sylvia A. Johnson, Series Editor**

*Translation of original text by Wesley M. Jacobsen*

*The publisher wishes to thank James E. Gerholdt, The Remarkable Reptiles, for his assistance in the preparation of this book.*

*Additional photographs provided by: pp. 8 (top), 9 (middle and bottom), 11 (bottom), 24 (left), 26 (left), 35, 36, 37, Barney Oldfield; pp. 8 (bottom), 10, 15, 31 (right), Klaus Paysan.*

*Illustrations by Takaji Matsui, Nagamasa Mukai, and Yooji Watanabe*

The glossary on page 46 gives definitions and pronunciations of words shown in **bold type** in the text.

*This book is available in two editions:*
Library binding by Lerner Publications Company
Soft cover by First Avenue Editions
241 First Avenue North
Minneapolis, Minnesota 55401

LIBRARY OF CONGRESS CATALOGING-IN-PUBLICATION DATA

**Johnson, Sylvia A.**
 Snakes.

 (A Lerner natural science book)
 Adaptation of: Hebi to tokage/Masuda Modoki.
 Includes index.
 Summary: Examines the physical characteristics
of snakes and the way in which they live.
  1. Snakes—Juvenile literature. I. Masuda, Modoki.
II. Masuda, Modoki. Hebi to tokage. III. Title.
IV. Series.
QL666.06J64  1986    597.96    86-7162
 ISBN 0-8225-1484-2 (lib. bdg.)
 ISBN 0-8225-9503-6 (pbk.)

International Standard Book Number: 0-8225-1484-2 (lib. bdg.)
International Standard Book Number: 0-8225-9503-6 (pbk.)
Library of Congress Catalog Number: 87-7162
Manufactured in the United States of America
10 11 12 13 14 15 – P/MP – 02 01 00 99 98 97

Snakes! The very word makes many people shudder with disgust and dread. They think of snakes as sneaky, slimy animals that pose a great danger to humans. When these snake-hating people walk in the woods, they imagine that there are snakes lying in wait under every rock and log, ready to slither out and attack the unwary hiker.

Although there are many people who view snakes with such dislike, there are many others who admire the animals for their beauty and grace or who even like them. After reading this book, we hope that you will find yourself in the second group of wise and understanding people who appreciate snakes.

Lizards like this skink (genus *Eumeces*) are members of the class Reptilia and closely related to snakes.

GETTING TO KNOW SNAKES

Who are these animals that cause such extreme reactions among humans? What kinds of creatures are they, and where do they fit into the animal kingdom?

Snakes are **reptiles**, members of the scientific class Reptilia. They are closely related to lizards, crocodiles, alligators, and turtles, all cold-blooded animals with scale- or plate-covered bodies. Although they have much in common with their relatives, snakes have one characteristic that makes them stand out in the class of reptiles: their long, slender bodies are without legs. (A few lizards are also legless, but most are four-legged creatures like the other reptiles.)

Snakes, lizards and other present-day reptiles are few in number and insignificant compared to the giant reptiles of the past. Millions of years ago, the dinosaurs, distant relatives of modern reptiles, dominated the world. Today, most reptiles are quiet, little-seen animals overshadowed by humans and other mammals that now rule the earth.

6

With its body looped gracefully around a tree branch, a snake quietly observes the world around it. A member of the large snake family Colubridae, this elegant reptile lives in Asia. It belongs to the genus *Elaphe*; its species name is *Elaphe climacophora*.

Garter snakes can be found in fields and woods in almost all parts of North America. These small striped reptiles are named after the brightly colored garters that men used to wear to hold up their socks. The species pictured here is *Thamnophis sirtalis,* the common garter snake.

## COLUBRIDS—COMMON SNAKES AROUND THE WORLD

The family Colubridae includes about 70 percent of all known kinds of snakes. Such familiar animals as garter snakes, water snakes, and rat snakes belong to this widespread family. Most colubrids are harmless, but a few are capable of administering a dose of poison, which is rarely fatal to humans.

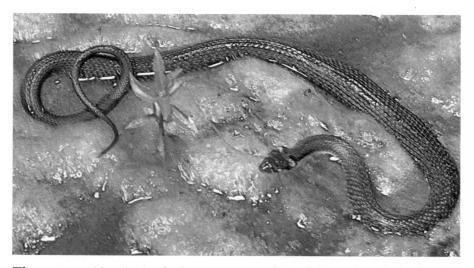

The genus *Natrix* includes many snakes that make their homes near water and feed on fish and frogs. This is the European water snake *(Natrix natrix)*, an excellent swimmer like all the other natrine snakes.

Members of the genus *Elaphe* are often called rat snakes because of their habit of feeding on rats and other rodents. These colubrids are common in many parts of Europe, Asia, and North America. Shown here is an Asian species, *Elaphe quadrivirgata.*

The beautiful blue racer *(Coluber constrictor)* is a North American snake noted for its swift movement. Other members of the genus *Coluber* inhabit Europe, Asia, and Africa.

Common in North America, the gentle milk snake *(Lampropeltis triangulum)* got its popular name because people used to believe that it drank milk from cows. Like many beliefs about snakes, this one is completely false.

## POISONOUS SNAKES—BEAUTIFUL BUT DANGEROUS

Only about 15 percent of all known snakes are poisonous. Most of these deadly snakes live in the tropical areas of the world, and they use their poison to get food or to defend themselves against attack.

There are several kinds of snake poison, or **venom**, and several methods of delivering it. These will be described in a later section of the book.

The viper family includes poisonous snakes that live in many parts of the world. Shown here is the European viper *(Vipera berus)*, also called the European adder. This snake belongs to the subfamily of true vipers. Its relatives pictured on the opposite page are all pit vipers, characterized by facial pits that function as sense organs.

Left: This Asian pit viper is the habu *(Trimeresurus flavoviridis)*. It lives on some of the Japanese islands, often near areas inhabited by people, and causes many human injuries each year. Right: The mamushi *(Agkistrodon halys)* is another pit viper found in several parts of Asia. It belongs to the same genus as the cottonmouth and copperhead snakes of North America.

The North American rattlesnakes are also pit vipers. They are famous for their dangerous bite and for the warning signal that they give by vibrating the horny segments on their tails. Shown here is the timber rattler, *Crotalus horridus*.

11

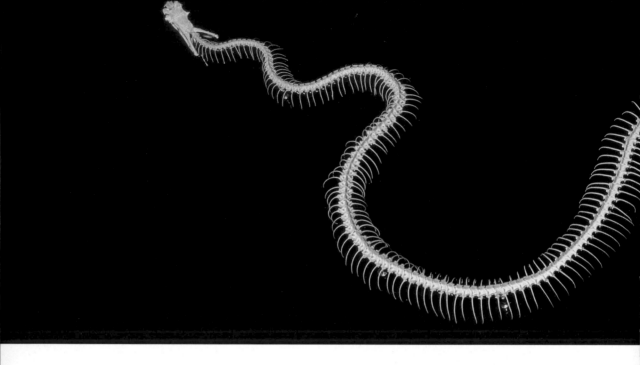

## A SNAKE'S BODY

The most conspicuous feature of a snake is its elongated, flexible, legless body. The bodies of snakes vary somewhat in size and shape; a few are thick and short, while others are as long and slender as a whip. In general, however, snakes have very "snaky" physical characteristics.

A snake's long body is supported by an equally long backbone, made up of as many as 400 vertebrae. (Humans have 33 vertebrae.) The vertebrae are joined to each other by flexible joints, which makes it possible for a snake to bend and twist its body easily.

Connected to each of a snake's vertebra is a pair of ribs.

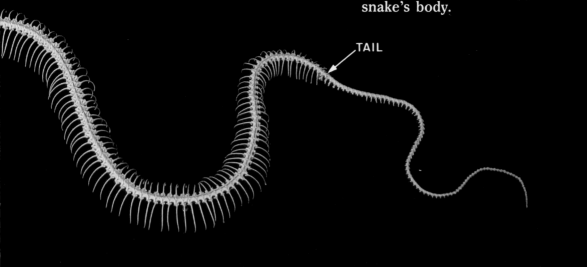

TAIL

Unlike the ribs of humans and most other vertebrate animals, snake ribs are not attached to a breastbone. Because of this, the rib structure can expand enormously, which, as you will discover, is a very useful characteristic.

A snake's body ends in a tail, although in looking at a living snake, it is sometimes difficult to know where the body ends and the tail begins. The tail is the part behind the anal opening, where waste material is expelled. Some kinds of snakes, like the species whose skeleton is shown above, have short tails. The tails of slender, tree-climbing snakes, on the other hand, can make up more than one-third of the animals' bodies.

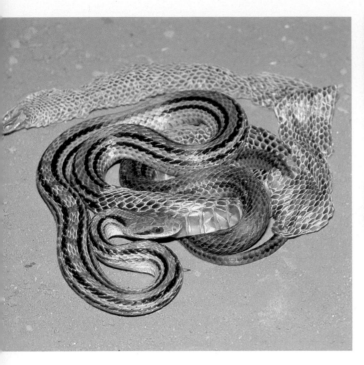

When a snake sheds its old skin, it peels it off inside out, like a long stocking (above). After shedding, the snake's colors glow brightly under a brand-new coat of transparent scales (left).

On the outside of a snake's long body is a covering of transparent, overlapping scales. Unlike fish scales, snake scales are part of the outer layer of the animal's skin. They make up a flexible, water-tight covering for the body.

A snake's coat of scales is flexible, but it does not grow along with the snake. As the reptile gets bigger, the outer layer of its skin must be replaced from time to time. The snake peels off its old skin by rubbing against rocks or twigs. Underneath is a new covering of perfectly fitted scales.

Contrary to popular belief, a snake's scaly coat does not feel wet or slimy. The animal's skin may glisten because of reflected light, but it is completely dry to the touch.

In this close-up photograph of a European water snake, you can see clearly the coat of overlapping scales that covers the reptile's body. Like many snakes, the water snake has a distinctive pattern of large scales on its head. The smaller body scales are keeled, with ridges running down their centers. Snakes with keeled scales have rougher coats than snakes with smooth scales.

The large scales on a snake's ventral side are attached to the body on only one side.

## GETTING AROUND WITHOUT LEGS

The scales on the upper, or dorsal, portion of a snake's body are small and form an intricate pattern. On the lower, or ventral, side of the body, there is usually just one row of large, thick scales that are attached to the body at only one edge. These ventral scales play an important role in a snake's movement.

Because they do not have legs, snakes cannot walk or run like other earthbound animals. Nevertheless, they have several very efficient methods of getting from place to place. One method, which scientists call **rectilinear creeping**, is often

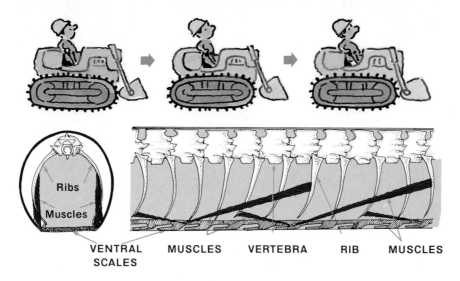

VENTRAL MUSCLES VERTEBRA RIB MUSCLES
SCALES

A snake's ventral scales are connected to its ribs by long muscles. When a snake moves by rectilinear creeping, the muscles raise groups of scales and thrust them forward. Then other muscles pull the scales backward, causing their edges to catch on the surface. This action propels the snake's body forward like a tractor moving over a caterpillar tread.

used by thick-bodied snakes like pythons. A creeping snake moves its body forward in a straight line by using its ventral scales something like the treads on a caterpillar tractor. The diagram above shows how this is done.

The most common form of snake locomotion is the graceful, flowing movement known, appropriately, as **serpentine movement** or **lateral undulation.** In this method, the snake uses its powerful muscles to produce a series of waves that move through its body from head to tail. Each wave or undulation pushes against obstacles on the surface, moving the snake forward. On a smooth surface such as a piece of glass, snakes have difficulty making any kind of progress.

Above: This snake is using serpentine locomotion to move over rough ground. Below: Snakes can also use serpentine movement to swim. The graceful undulations of their bodies push against the water to create forward motion.

A snake uses concertina movement to climb straight up a stone wall.

Another method of snake locomotion is called **concertina movement**. A snake moving in this way uses its body something like the "squeeze box" of a concertina or accordian, alternately compressing and expanding it. Climbing the trunk of a tree in concertina style, the snake stretches out the front part of its body while keeping the back part in tight loops. Then it compresses the front end and pulls the tail end forward. By repeating this movement, a snake can inch its way up a tree with ease.

Some snakes that live in desert areas have a special way of moving called **sidewinding**. This peculiar method of locomotion allows the reptiles to make their way over loose, shifting sand.

**SERPENTINE MOVEMENT**

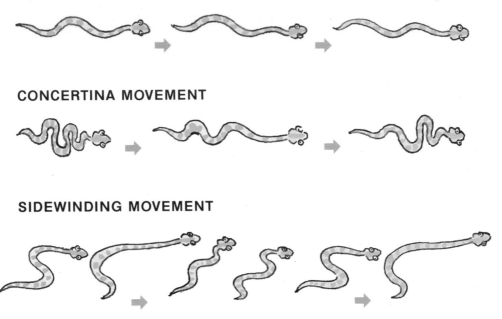

**CONCERTINA MOVEMENT**

**SIDEWINDING MOVEMENT**

Instead of moving forward, a sidewinding snake proceeds through a series of sideways movements. Keeping its head and tail on the ground, the reptile raises its midsection and moves it to the side. Then it moves its head and tail into position with the rest of its body. The sidewinding movement of such snakes as the American sidewinder (a rattlesnake) and the African horned viper creates a series of distinctive J-shaped marks in the sands of their desert homes.

Opposite: Like this Asian keeled snake (genus *Rhabdophis*), many snakes move as easily through the branches of a tree as they do on the ground.

When a snake is ready to shed, its eye scales become cloudy (left). As the old skin is peeled off, the snake's lidless eye is revealed under a new transparent covering (right).

## A SNAKE'S SENSES

Snakes manage to move very well even though they are without legs. They are also able to perceive the world around them through senses that are rather different from the ones used by humans and other animals.

Snakes do have some of the same kinds of sense organs as we do. They have eyes, although their vision is not very acute. A snake's eyes are never closed because they do not have lids. A clear lens-like scale protects each eye from injury. When a snake sheds its skin, its eye scales come off with the other scales and are replaced by new coverings.

Snakes have no external ears or eardrums, but they do seem to have a limited sense of hearing. Vibrations are transmitted through the bones of their heads to the tiny bones of the inner ears. In this way, snakes may be able to sense the movements of prey animals near them.

One of a snake's most important sense organs is its long, forked tongue. Snakes have little sense of taste. Instead, their tongues, along with their nostrils, help them to smell the world around them.

When a snake darts out its forked tongue, it picks up scent particles from the air and ground. When the tongue is returned to the snake's mouth, its tip enters **Jacobson's organ,** a special structure made up of two hollow sacs in the roof of the mouth. This unique organ is lined with nerve endings that respond to odors. The nerves communicate with the snake's brain, providing important information about its environment.

A snake's forked tongue (left) picks up scent particles that are transferred to a special organ inside the reptile's mouth (right).

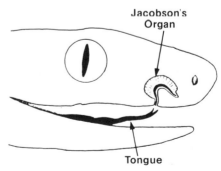

Jacobson's Organ

Tongue

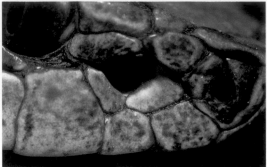

Left: **In this photograph, you can see one of the pit organs of a typical pit viper, the timber rattlesnake.** Above: A close-up of a facial pit.

All snakes pick up odors with their tongues. Some snakes have special sense organs that react to heat. The group of snakes known as **pit vipers** (part of the family Viperidae) is famous for its heat-sensitive **pit organs.**

Pit vipers such as rattlesnakes often hunt at night, when eyesight is of little use in finding prey. Instead, these snakes locate warm-blooded animals like rodents by means of the heat-sensitive pits on their heads.

These pits are lined with nerves that react to changes in temperature. When a hunting snake comes near a small animal, its body heat registers on the sensitive nerves. By moving its head from side to side, the snake can locate and seize its prey on even the darkest night.

Pit vipers are not the only snakes with pit organs. Many pythons and boas, members of the family Boidae, have rows of pits above their mouths that react to heat in a similar way.

24

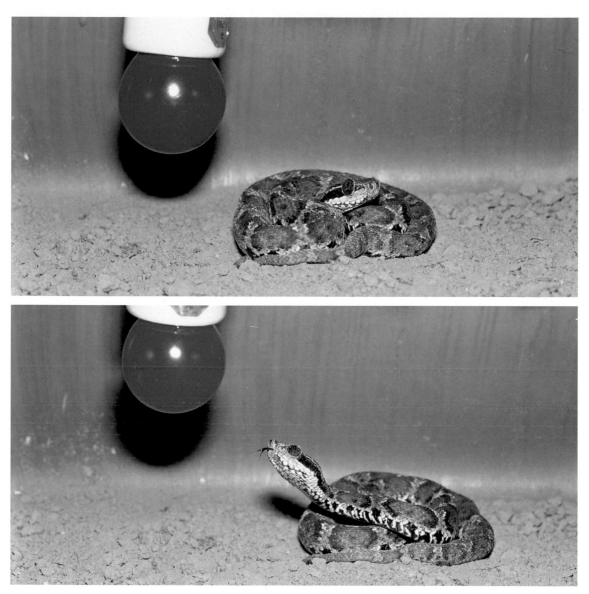

These two photographs demonstrate the acuteness of a pit viper's special sense organs. In the upper photograph, the snake, whose eyes are covered, is unaware of the light bulb near it. The lower photograph shows the animal's reaction when the light is turned on. It immediately senses the heat produced by the bulb and moves toward it.

Left: **Like all members of the genus** *Elaphe,* **this beautiful corn snake kills its prey by constriction.** Above: **A constricting snake tightens its coils around a mouse until the animal dies of suffocation.**

## HUNTING AND EATING

With their acute specialized senses, snakes are well-equipped for their lives as predators. All snakes are meat-eaters, and they spend many hours of the day or night hunting for food.

Most snakes feed on small animals like birds, frogs, toads, rabbits, and mice. Some snakes specialize in eating eggs or even other snakes. Hunting snakes wait in ambush or track their prey, using their sensitive tongues to pick up a scent trail. When they find a potential meal, many snakes lunge at the animal and seize it in their mouths. The prey is swallowed whole and alive.

Some snakes kill animals before consuming them. Poisonous snakes use their venom as a weapon. **Constricting** snakes like pythons wrap coils of their powerful bodies around their

prey. The predators squeeze the animals until they die of suffocation. Then the snakes begin the long process of getting their meals into their stomachs.

Above and opposite: **A snake swallowing a chicken egg. Like some other snakes that eat eggs, this species** *(Elaphe climacophora)* **has special sharp spines on its neck vertebrae that pierce the egg shell inside its body. The snake consumes the contents of the egg and eliminates the crushed shell.**

Regardless of how they catch prey, all snakes swallow their food whole. A snake's small, pointed teeth are not designed for tearing or chewing, only for holding. In order to eat, the snake must get the whole prey animal through its mouth and into its body.

A snake's body is specially designed for this task. Its skin is flexible and can stretch easily. The ribs, attached only to the backbone, can be spread wide to accommodate the prey's body. But how can a slender snake get its mouth around a fat rat or a large egg like the one being devoured in the photographs on this page? This amazing feat is possible because of the unique design of a snake's jaw and skull bones.

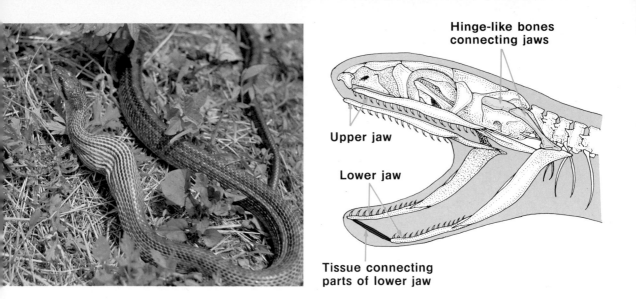

Hinge-like bones connecting jaws

Upper jaw

Lower jaw

Tissue connecting parts of lower jaw

The upper and lower jaws are joined by hinge-like bones that allow a snake to open its mouth very wide. Each side of the two jaws can be moved separately so that a snake can "walk" its mouth around a prey animal, first moving one side forward and then the other. Its sharp teeth slant backward, gripping the prey and preventing it from escaping. Large amounts of saliva are produced in the mouth and throat, helping the snake's meal to go down easier.

It may take almost an hour for a snake to swallow a large animal. To continue breathing during this time, a snake extends its windpipe out the bottom of its mouth and takes in oxygen through this well-protected tube.

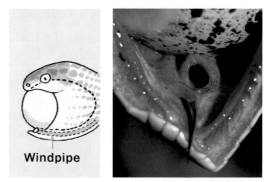

Windpipe

## VENOM—A DEADLY WEAPON

In their careers as predators, some snakes make use of a deadly weapon—venom. A dose of venom can quickly paralyze a prey animal and take its life without a struggle.

There are several groups of poisonous snakes, each with its own special method of killing. Vipers, members of the family Viperidae, are probably the most highly developed of the venomous reptiles. Pit vipers and their relatives, the true vipers, have two long, hollow fangs in their upper jaws. These fangs are attached to bones that swivel or rotate.

When a viper's mouth is closed, the fangs are folded back against the roof of the mouth. When the snake is ready to strike, it opens its mouth wide and the fangs swing into a vertical position, at a right angle to the jaw bone.

An attacking viper lunges at its prey with open mouth, stabbing the animal with its sharp fangs. Venom from the snake's venom glands flows through the hollow fangs and into the victim's body. The venom of many vipers contains substances called **hemotoxins** that cause tissue damage and internal bleeding.

A viper bite is dangerous but not always deadly, depending on the size of the victim and the amount of venom injected. Humans bitten by a viper such as a rattlesnake often recover if they are given an **antitoxin** that counteracts the damaging effects of the snake's venom.

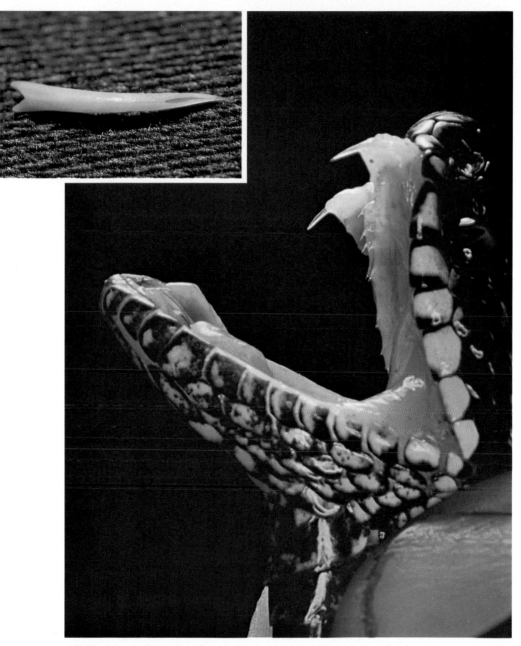

With its mouth open, a European viper reveals its long, deadly fangs. In the small photograph, you can clearly see the hollow shaft and sharp point of a viper fang.

A VIPER'S FANGS

AN ELAPID'S FANGS

This poisonous reptile is an Asian coral snake (genus *Calliophis*). Like its distant relatives, the coral snakes of North and South America, it is an elapid, with short fangs fixed in its upper jaw.

Another large group of venomous snakes is made up of **elapids,** members of the family Elapidae. In this group are the famous cobras of Asia and Africa, as well as the beautiful but dangerous coral snakes of North and South America.

Elapids are not quite as efficient in delivering poison as the vipers. Because their fangs are fixed in position on the upper jaw, they are much shorter than those of vipers and incapable of causing as deep a wound. Many elapids, however, have very powerful venom, and even a little is enough to kill an animal. Elapid venom often contains **neurotoxins** that attack the nervous system, affecting the function of the heart and lungs.

The elapids and the vipers include most of the world's poisonous snakes, but there are a few other kinds of deadly serpents. Sea snakes, members of the family Hydrophiidae, are related to the elapids and have similar kinds of fangs.

32

These unaggressive snakes live in the warm waters of the Pacific Ocean and use their venom to catch the fish on which they feed.

Among the generally harmless colubrid snakes are some venomous species. The fangs of these snakes are in the backs of their jaws, and they are not hollow but grooved. **Rear-fanged snakes** cannot inject venom like other poisonous snakes; most of them have to chew on their prey in order to get venom into their bodies. For this reason, rear-fanged snakes are not usually considered a serious threat to humans. One member of the group, however, the boomslang of Africa *(Dispholidus typus)*, has powerful venom and the ability to strike quickly and effectively.

This large sea snake (genus *Laticauda*) spends most of its time in the coastal waters of the eastern Pacific Ocean. It comes on land only to lay its eggs.

Animals that prey on snakes include large birds like hawks (left) and other reptiles such as this colorful Asian snake, a member of the genus *Dinodon* (right).

## DEFENSE AGAINST ENEMIES

Poisonous snakes use their venom to kill animals for food, but they also employ this deadly weapon in self-defense. Many snakes are the prey of other predators, and they need all the help they can get to avoid being killed and eaten.

Large birds like eagles, hawks, and owls are among the most important predators of snakes. One of these raptors can swoop down from the sky and seize a snake in its powerful claws before the animal can escape or defend itself by striking.

High on the list of snake predators are other snakes. Certain kinds of snakes like the king snake specialize in feeding on smaller snakes. Some of these predators are immune to their prey's venom and can attack vipers and other poisonous snakes without danger of being bitten.

Of all the creatures that prey on snakes, humans are probably the biggest threat. Some people will kill any snake that they see, even if the animal poses no danger to them. This extreme and unreasonable reaction has led to the killing of many harmless snakes as well as those that benefit the human world by eating rodents and other pests.

Like its larger relatives, the massausauga (genus *Sistrurus*) or pigmy rattler uses its rattle to warn potential enemies to stay away.

For most kinds of snakes, concealment and flight are the most common methods of self-defense against enemies. Both poisonous and nonpoisonous reptiles will do their best to avoid trouble if they possibly can.

In an effort to frighten away an attacker, this hognose snake *(Heterodon platyrhinos)* has raised its upper body and expanded its neck. The hognose also makes a loud hissing sound when threatened.

If they are cornered, many snakes will try to frighten away potential attackers. The rattlesnake's famous rattle is often used to warn an enemy of the snake's presence and its willingness to strike. When threatened, nonpoisonous snakes like king snakes sometimes vibrate their tails against the ground to make a sound very much like the rattlesnake's warning signal.

Another method that snakes use to scare away attackers is to make themselves look as large and threatening as possible. Hooded snakes like cobras are experts at this technique. They raise the upper parts of their bodies and spread the ribs below their heads to create wide hoods. Smaller, less dangerous snakes like the North American hognose snake also expand their necks to make themselves look larger and more threatening to attackers.

If all its other self-defense techniques fail, a hognose snake will try to discourage a predator by playing dead.

The hognose snake, a small animal with a turned-up snout used for burrowing, is one of the champions of self-defense in the snake world. If its puffing-up act doesn't work, the hognose will often play dead to discourage a predator. It will flop over on its back and go limp, with its mouth open and its tongue hanging out. This snake is so persistent in its attempt to fool an attacker that it will flop over again and continue playing dead even after being turned right-side up.

Like snakes, lizards are cold-blooded animals whose body temperatures are controlled by their environments.

## A LIFE CONTROLLED BY THE SEASONS

All the activities of a snake's life—hunting, defense against enemies, seeking a mate—are influenced by one very important factor, and that is the weather. The lives of all animals are shaped in some way by the climate of their environment. For **cold-blooded** creatures like snakes and other reptiles, however, variations in temperature are matters of life and death.

Snakes, lizards, and their relatives do not actually have cold blood. Instead, the temperatures of their blood systems and all their other body parts are controlled by the temperature of the environment. The scientific name for this condition is **ectothermic,** which means "heated from outside." Mammals and birds are **endotherms,** creatures whose body temperatures are controlled from inside.

To maintain the proper body temperature, a snake must behave in a certain way. It must hide from the intense midday sun that would raise its temperature too high and bring death. In cool weather, on the other hand, a snake will bask in the sun to keep its body functioning.

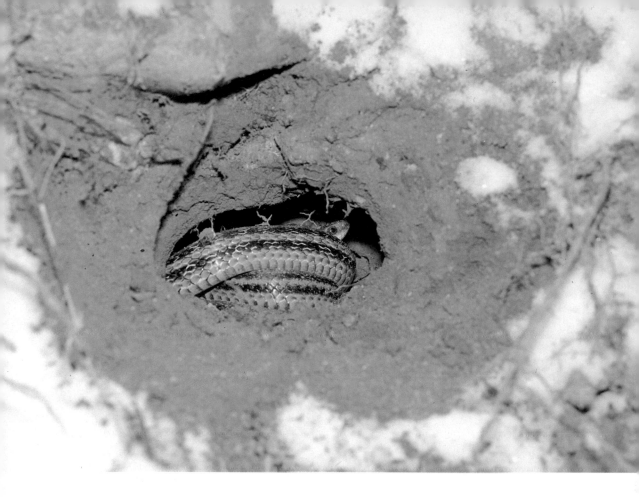

For snakes that live in temperate climates, the long, cold winter is the most dangerous time of the year. To avoid freezing to death, these snakes **hibernate** during the winter months. They seek shelter in burrows, hollows, or caves where the temperature stays above freezing. Sometimes alone, sometimes in groups, hibernating snakes spend the winter in a state of inactivity, during which all their body systems slow down. Only when the spring sun brings renewed warmth will they resume their active lives.

In spring, hibernating snakes return to life slowly. At first they stay near their dens, soaking in the reviving rays of the spring sun. As soon as their bodies are back to normal, however, they are ready to begin an important job—mating and producing young.

Above: A female snake (top) usually has a shorter tail than a male of the same species (bottom). The male's tail is broader at the base because the animal's reproductive organs are located there. Right: A male and female snake twine their bodies together during mating.

Most male snakes find appropriate mates by using their acute senses of smell. Their forked tongues pick up special odors produced by female snakes during the mating season. When a male has located a willing partner of his species, the two snakes twine their bodies together, and the male's sperm cells pass into the female's body.

After they have finished mating, the two animals part to live their separate lives during the warm months of spring and summer. Inside the female's reproductive system, however, new life has begun to develop.

The females of many snake species produce young that are encased in eggs. Referred to as **oviparous,** these egg-laying snakes include such familiar kinds as milk snakes, pythons, and coral snakes. Other snakes give birth to live young; among these **viviparous** snakes are boas, pit vipers, and garter snakes.

41

A female snake laying eggs. Snake eggs are long and narrow, with flexible, leathery shells.

Most oviparous snakes lay their eggs in early summer, a month or so after mating. The eggs, numbering anywhere from 2 to over 100, are deposited in piles of rotting wood or leaves and left to develop on their own, warmed by the heat of the summer sun. Live-bearing females carry the developing young snakes inside their bodies for most of the summer. They give birth in August or September, just about the same time that the eggs of the oviparous females are ready to hatch.

Right: A baby pit viper being born. The little snake emerges from its mother's body encased in a transparent membrane, which it quickly breaks. Below: Snakes hatched from eggs use a special egg tooth on their upper jaws to cut through the leathery shells. This tooth falls off soon after hatching.

Soon after they are born or hatch from their eggs, young snakes are ready to take care of themselves.

Whether they emerge from eggs or from their mothers' bodies, baby snakes are on their own as soon as they enter the world. They may stay near their mothers for a while after birth or hatching, but they are not given any aid or care. Soon the young snakes begin wandering off to find food. Even at this early stage, they are able to catch small prey, killing it by constriction or an injection of venom, depending on their species.

Snakes hatched or born in early autumn have only a short time to prepare for the period of winter hibernation that is soon to come. They must eat enough food to supply the energy that their bodies will need throughout the long months of inactivity. As winter approaches, the young snakes instinctively look for shelters that will protect them from the deadly cold.

44

A snake warms itself in the golden light of the autumn sun. Soon it will be winter, and the reptile will enter the silent, sunless world of hibernation.

# GLOSSARY

**antitoxin**—a drug that counteracts the effects of a poison such as snake venom

**cold-blooded**—having a body temperature that is controlled by the temperature of the environment

**colubrids (KUHL-uh-brihds)**—snakes belonging to the large family Colubridae

**concertina movement**—a form of locomotion in which a snake alternately compresses and stretches out its body. Concertina movement is often used in climbing trees.

**constricting**—tightening a snake's coils around a prey animal until it dies of suffocation

**ectothermic (ehk-tuh-THER-mik)**—having a body temperature controlled by the temperature of the environment. Animals with this kind of physical system are called **ectotherms (EHK-tuh-therms)**.

**egg tooth**—a special tooth on the upper jaw of a reptile used to break out of the egg shell at hatching

**elapids (EL-ah-pihds)**—poisonous snakes in the family Elapidae

**endotherms**—animals whose body temperatures are controlled from within

**hemotoxins (hem-uh-TAHK-sins)**—snake venoms that affect the functioning of the blood system

**hibernate**—to spend the winter in a state of inactivity, during which body temperature drops and heartbeat and respiration slow down

**Jacobson's organ**—an organ in a snake's head made up of two sacs lined with nerve endings sensitive to odors

**keel**—a ridge that runs down the center of a snake scale. Many snakes have keeled scales on their bodies.

**lateral undulation (LAT-uh-ruhl un-dew-LAY-shun)**—a method of movement in which a snake uses its muscles to produce a series of waves that run through its body

**neurotoxins (nyur-uh-TAHK-sins)**—snake venoms that affect the functioning of the nervous system

**oviparous (o-VIP-uh-rehs)**—producing young that hatch from eggs

**pit organs**—depressions on a snake's head lined with nerves sensitive to heat

**pit vipers**—members of the family Viperidae characterized by facial pits

**rear-fanged snakes**—poisonous colubrid snakes with grooved fangs in the rear of their mouths

**rectilinear (rek-tih-LIN-ee-uhr) creeping**—a method of movement in which a snake keeps its body straight and moves forward by pushing on the ground with its large ventral scales

**reptiles**—snakes, lizards, crocodiles, and other members of the scientific class Reptilia

**serpentine (SUR-puhn-tine) movement**—another name for lateral undulation

**sidewinding**—a method of movement used by desert snakes in which the head and tail serve as supports while the middle of the body is moved sideways

**venom (VEN-uhm)**—the poison used by certain snakes to capture prey or to defend themselves against enemies

**viviparous (vih-VIP-uh-rehs)**—producing living young

# INDEX

TOWN OF SMITHFIELD

JUNIOR HIGH SCHOOL